Ashton Kutcher

Ashton Kutcher

Other books in the People in the News series:

Beyoncé

Jamie Foxx

Angelina Jolie

Avril Lavigne

Tobey McGuire

Barack Obama

JK Rowling

Hilary Swank

Usher

people in the NEWS

Ashton Kutcher

by Terri Dougherty

LUCENT BOOKS
An imprint of Thomson Gale, a part of The Thomson Corporation

THOMSON
★
™
GALE

Detroit • New York • San Francisco • San Diego • New Haven, Conn.
Waterville, Maine • London • Munich

For more information, contact:
Lucent Books
27500 Drake Rd.
Farmington Hills, MI 48331-3535
Or you can visit our Internet site at http://www.gale.com

LIBRARY OF CONGRESS CATALOGING-IN-PUBLICATION DATA

Dougherty, Terri.
    Ashton Kutcher / by Terri Dougherty.
        p. cm. — (People in the news)
    Includes bibliographical references.
    Contents: Iowa upbringing—Fresh face in Hollywood—Making dimness pay—Producer—New projects, new relationship—Settling in.
        ISBN 1-59018-718-0 (hard cover : alk. paper) 1. Kutcher, Ashton, 1978– —Juvenile literature. 2. Actors—United States—Biography—Juvenile literature. I. Title. II. Series: People in the news (San Diego, Calif.)
    PN2287.K88D68 2006
    792.02'8092--dc22

                                                                        2006005100

Printed in China

Contents

Foreword 8

Introduction 10
Driven to Succeed

Chapter 1 14
Iowa Upbringing

Chapter 2 25
Fresh Face in Hollywood

Chapter 3 36
Making Dimness Pay

Chapter 4 49
Producer

Chapter 5 63
New Projects, New Relationship

Chapter 6 76
Settling In

Notes 91

Important Dates 95

For Further Reading 97

Index 99

Picture Credits 103

About the Author 104

F ame and celebrity are alluring. People are drawn to those who walk in fame's spotlight, whether they are known for great accomplishments or for notorious deeds. The lives of the famous pique public interest and attract attention, perhaps because their experiences seem in some ways so different from, yet in other ways so similar to, our own.

Newspapers, magazines, and television regularly capitalize on this fascination with celebrity by running profiles of famous people. For example, television programs such as *Entertainment Tonight* devote all of their programming to stories about entertainment and entertainers. Magazines such as *People* fill their pages with stories of the private lives of famous people. Even newspapers, newsmagazines, and television news frequently delve into the lives of well-known personalities. Despite the number of articles and programs, few provide more than a superficial glimpse at their subjects.

Lucent's People in the News series offers young readers a deeper look into the lives of today's newsmakers, the influences that have shaped them, and the impact they have had in their fields of endeavor and on other people's lives. The subjects of the series hail from many disciplines and walks of life. They include authors, musicians, athletes, political leaders, entertainers, entrepreneurs, and others who have made a mark on modern life and who, in many cases, will continue to do so for years to come.

These biographies are more than factual chronicles. Each book emphasizes the contributions, accomplishments, or deeds that have brought fame or notoriety to the individual and shows how that person has influenced modern life. Authors portray their subjects in a realistic, unsentimental light. For example, Bill Gates—the cofounder and chief executive officer of the software giant Microsoft—has been instrumental in making personal computers the most vital tool of the modern age. Few dispute his business savvy, his perseverance, or his technical expertise, yet critics say he is ruthless in his dealings with competitors and driven more by his desire to maintain Microsoft's dominance in the computer industry than by an interest in furthering technology.

In these books, young readers will encounter inspiring stories about real people who achieved success despite enormous obstacles. Oprah Winfrey—the most powerful, most watched, and wealthiest woman on television today—spent the first six years of her life in the care of her grandparents while her unwed mother sought work and a better life elsewhere. Her adolescence was colored by promiscuity, pregnancy at age fourteen, rape, and sexual abuse.

Each author documents and supports his or her work with an array of primary and secondary source quotations taken from diaries, letters, speeches, and interviews. All quotes are footnoted to show readers exactly how and where biographers derive their information and provide guidance for further research. The quotations enliven the text by giving readers eyewitness views of the life and accomplishments of each person covered in the People in the News series.

In addition, each book in the series includes photographs, annotated bibliographies, timelines, and comprehensive indexes. For both the casual reader and the student researcher, the People in the News series offers insight into the lives of today's newsmakers—people who shape the way we live, work, and play in the modern age.

Driven to Succeed

Ashton Kutcher may be best known for his handsome features and the jokes he plays on his celebrity friends, but there is much more to the actor and producer than good looks and practical jokes. He dreamed of being an actor while he was growing up in Iowa, but never thought his dreams would be realized. Yet success and achievement came quickly to Kutcher, whose drive and desire to succeed were coupled early on with some fortunate breaks. Throughout his career, Kutcher has showed a knack for capitalizing on those breaks, as well as an impressive work ethic.

Although he harbored youthful hopes of becoming an actor, Kutcher did not dwell on this idea when he was growing up. He did not think acting would be a practical career choice, and could not even envision getting started. Then a chance meeting led to a win in a modeling competition, and the unexpected modeling career opened the door to a career in television. Kutcher's career was jump-started by a string of lucky breaks, but he made the most of them by keeping his head and not being swayed by the glamour of the entertainment business.

Kutcher's personality is much more thoughtful and perceptive than the roles he portrayed early in his career, when he made his mark by playing dim-witted, goofy characters. While Kutcher does have a humorous side, the trait stems from his cleverness and an ability to laugh at himself, not naïveté. While his roles in *That '70s Show* and *Dude, Where's My Car?* led some to expect the same simpleminded silliness from Kutcher himself, the onetime biochemical engineering student had a surprise for them: He is focused, intelligent, and a quick study. Although his looks got him his first break, Kutcher was smart enough to develop skills that would help him succeed in multiple areas of the entertainment business.

Kutcher is aware of what his gifts could best accomplish and has a canny knack for realizing what is possible. He has learned how to work within the system to find roles that suit him, and has become a producer of television shows such as *Punk'd*. While Kutcher's acting has not always received rave reviews, he has bolstered his career by learning more about the business side of Hollywood. Producing movies and television shows has given

A 2004 photo of Ashton Kutcher shows the good looks that won the hearts of young movie audiences.

him another outlet for his creativity. As a result, he has been able to consistently keep his name in the mix, even when his movies receive less than stellar reviews.

The opinions of others have never been of great concern to Kutcher, however. He is not afraid to annoy celebrities with the gags on *Punk'd,* and risked crossing the line of tastefulness with the show *Beauty and the Geek.* He does not want to harm anyone, but at the same time is not afraid to point out others' foibles as he encourages them not to take themselves too seriously.

Looking more like a contestant than the producer of Beauty and the Geek, *a bearded and bespectacled Kutcher poses with the first show's contestants and crew.*

Kutcher has tried hard to follow that advice himself, as he tries to keep his career and personal life in perspective. He tries not to get caught up in the celebrity world, even as he makes the necessary appearances at movie premieres and does the media interviews required of a star. It is not easy for him to keep his personal life private, as his relationship with and marriage to actress Demi Moore, fifteen years his senior and the mother of three daughters, has made him a favorite target of celebrity gossip magazines. Kutcher was already a popular figure in the media because of his good looks, and his relationship with Moore only intensified the interest.

The actor and producer takes the attention in stride, however. He prefers to concentrate on his acting, producing, and family life rather than what is being said about him. He has proven that he can accomplish much more than people expect from him, and is always looking for new ventures. Kutcher's career has been marked by persistence and hard work, and those traits continue to prevail as he pursues new goals and enjoys life with his family.

Chapter 1

Iowa Upbringing

Ashton Kutcher's childhood was both comfortable and difficult. He grew up in a pleasant rural area and had parents who loved and cared for him. However, there was tension at home. Ashton coped with serious family problems by staying busy, but inner struggles emerged as he matured.

As he entered his late teens, Ashton began to feel out of step with his small community. He craved a broader view of the world and began to feel confined by what he perceived as a narrow point of view. While he loved those he was closest to, he did not feel Iowa was the place for him. At the same time, it did not seem possible to simply leave. These conflicting conditions made him restless and left him looking for a way to broaden his horizons.

Childhood in Cedar Rapids

The uncertain teenager who was to become famous as Ashton Kutcher was born Christopher Ashton Kutcher on February 7, 1978, in Cedar Rapids, Iowa. His twin brother, Michael, was born five minutes after Ashton. The day of their birth was one of both happiness and anxiety for their parents, Larry and Diane. While Ashton was born healthy, his brother was not. Michael would later be diagnosed with mild cerebral palsy and would require medical attention during his childhood.

The Kutcher twins had a sister, Tausha, who was three years older, and the siblings spent their childhood in Cedar Rapids, a city of about 120,000 people. The east-central Iowa community prides itself on a climate with four distinct seasons and opportunities to enjoy all of them. Agriculture and manufacturing are the two main industries in the area, and a number of the businesses deal with food products. Larry Kutcher worked in a General Mills factory that turned grain into breakfast cereal. Diane Kutcher worked in nearby Iowa City, at a Procter & Gamble plant that made shampoo and other health and beauty products.

Larry and Diane Kutcher worked hard and tried to create a stable environment for their children, but they could not hide the strain in their relationship. Their children could not help but notice their arguments.

Ashton loved his family and those around him. His parents' contentious relationship bothered him, however, and he did not want to be drawn into their arguments. "I saw some stuff I probably shouldn't have seen," he says, "and didn't want to be involved, and I didn't want to have to take a side."[1] When the twins were thirteen, their parents divorced.

Kutcher, his twin brother, and their older sister spent their childhood in Cedar Rapids, Iowa (pictured).

Health Concerns

Another crisis hit the Kutcher family the year the twins turned thirteen: Michael contracted a virus and developed myocarditis. The disorder inflamed his heart and endangered his life.

Ashton was troubled by his brother's illness. He hesitated to go home after school because he did not want to hear more bad news. He frequently visited Michael in the hospital during this difficult time, even though it pained him to see his brother so sick. "He showed me the love one brother has for another," Michael says.[2]

Michael's condition was very serious, and he required a heart transplant. Ashton so badly wanted his brother's life to be saved that he wished he could give him his own heart. He even thought about jumping off a hospital balcony. As Larry Kutcher was working to convince his healthy son that ending his own life was not the way to save his brother, doctors rushed out to announce that they had a heart for Michael.

The transplant saved Michael's life. It also made an impression on his twin, leading Ashton to think about a career in medical research. He wanted to find a cure for the virus that almost claimed his brother's life.

Getting That Rock Star Feeling

To avoid constantly thinking about his brother's health and his parents' divorce, Ashton became active in after-school activities. As a seventh grader he was small for his age and not certain he had enough athletic ability to participate in sports. Instead, he tried out for a play.

His first onstage experience was in *The Crying Princess and the Golden Goose*. He played a thief in the play about a king who is so eager to get his daughter to stop crying that he offers gold and the princess's hand in marriage to the person who can make her laugh. The simple children's play sealed Ashton's love for acting. Being in front of an audience gave him an adrenaline rush. He felt like a rock star, and his dream of being an actor was born.

Kirk Cameron, a costar on the hit show Growing Pains, *was an inspiration to Kutcher.*

Ashton's interest in acting was also stimulated by shows he watched on television. He enjoyed *The Cosby Show, Diff'rent Strokes,* and *Roseanne,* but the actor who inspired him most was Kirk Cameron. In the late 1980s and early 1990s, Cameron played teenager Mike Seaver on the sitcom *Growing Pains* and had a large fan base of young teens. To be an actor like Cameron,

Brother's Compliment

When Ashton became a successful model and then an actor, there was one person who was not surprised. Ashton's brother, Michael, said his twin had long attracted notice for his looks. "He's always been good looking, always got the girl," Michael Kutcher says.

Although Ashton recalls being rather awkward socially in high school, his brother says Ashton was the more social of the pair. He also notes that his brother was protective of him. "He's more outgoing and energetic than I am," Michael says. "He always stood up for me."

Quoted in *People*, "Spirit of '76," November 2, 1998, p. 75.

Ashton's good looks and winning ways were praised by his brother.

who played a funny, popular teen on a TV show, seemed like the ideal career.

Acting was not Ashton's only interest, however. He did not forget how helpless he felt when his brother was hospitalized and close to death. He also pursued an interest in science, spurred on by thoughts of one day finding a cure for the virus that had caused his brother's heart to weaken. With his brother's health in mind, Ashton put effort into his schoolwork. He still dreamed of acting, but his practical nature told him it was probably not a realistic career path for a kid from Iowa.

Homestead

In 1993 Diane Kutcher moved with her children to Homestead, about 25 miles (40km) south of Cedar Rapids. The tiny community, with a population of a few hundred people, was about 20 miles (32km) from Iowa City, where the Procter & Gamble plant was located. It was also close enough to Cedar Rapids that the children could easily visit their father. In Homestead Diane built a home with construction worker Mark Portwood, whom she would marry in 1996.

In little Homestead, it seemed that everyone knew everyone else. To the teenage Ashton, it seemed that one of the town's main sources of entertainment was keeping track of what others were doing. "The worst thing was that in my town, everyone had a police scanner, and for kicks, they'd sit around and listen to who was getting in trouble," he says. "My parents knew if I'd been caught speeding before I even walked in the door."[3]

While this MTV audience obviously idolizes Kutcher, the actor has confessed that he was not popular in high school.

Not Part of the "In" Crowd

Ashton rode the bus to Clear Creek Amana High School in Tiffin, about 12 miles (19km) away from Homestead. In high school, he was not part of the popular crowd. Still thin and small in stature, he felt like a geek. "Junior high and high school are the most terrifying years of your life," he says. "Your body is out of whack. You realize that girls exist, but they want nothing to do with you."[4]

Although somewhat uncomfortable among his peers, Ashton did not keep to himself. In addition to singing in the choir, he took up athletics, playing football and joining the wrestling team. He wrestled in some of the lightest wrestling weight classes: 103 pounds (47kg) as a freshman, 112 pounds (51kg) as a sophomore, and 119 (54kg) as a junior.

Feelings of social ineptness vanished in the classroom, however. He put effort into his homework and earned As in many subjects, as his brother's illness and recovery continued to inspire him to work hard.

Ashton worked outside school as well. In a farming community there are always plenty of jobs. Ashton helped area farmers bale hay and take care of cattle. He also volunteered at his church. He taught younger students and encouraged them to relate what they were learning to their own lives. "It was more about: 'How do you create a miracle in your life? What can you do to make your life better?'" he says. "It was important to me to encourage the kids there that it really is not about something that happened many thousands of years ago, that it's really about something that's happening now."[5]

Growth Spurt

During his senior year in high school Ashton suddenly stopped being one of the smallest kids in school. In one year he grew 6 inches (15cm) and gained 50 pounds (23kg), eventually reaching 6 foot 2½ inches (1.9m). This presented a new problem. He was outgrowing his clothing faster than his parents could afford to replace it. As a result, his jeans were sometimes unfashionably short.

Although he was no longer shorter than his classmates and had a girlfriend his senior year, Ashton still did not feel that he fit in. Because of the clothes he wore, some students ridiculed him. "Other kids made up a mean song about my lame shoes," he says. "I have been uncool my entire life."[6]

Breaking Out

Ashton was a model student through most of high school. He worked hard, concentrated on his schoolwork, and followed the rules. In his senior year, however, he began to question why he was working so hard. He expected more to come of his hard work and thought he was not being sufficiently praised for being a good

The Joke's on Ashton

Ashton Kutcher became a professional prankster after he made it to Hollywood, but while he was growing up in Iowa he was sometimes the object of his sister's practical jokes. While Ashton was sleeping, his older sister, Tausha, would sometimes put makeup on his face. "Can you imagine how scary that was for a little kid, to wake up with lipstick, eye shadow and mascara?" he asks.

Ashton says his family did not hesitate to laugh when a family member made a mistake. "It's healthy to make fun of yourself," he says. "I come from a family where if you do something stupid, they're on you immediately about it. So you learn to bail yourself out before they can bail you. If I can make fun of myself before you can make fun of me, I win."

Quoted in *People,* "Ashton Kutcher: Actor," May 12, 2003, p. 78; and Nancy Mills, "Prankster with Pull," *New York Daily News,* January 18, 2004. www.nydailynews.com/entertainmentstory/155366p-136565c.html.

kid. He did not see how his exemplary behavior was benefiting him.

He did not feel he could talk to anyone about his frustrations, and as they intensified he started behaving badly as a way of venting. "That stuff started to build up inside of me. And when you hold it in, that's when you start to get into trouble—and that's what I did," he says. "I was trying to do the right thing all the time and I felt like it wasn't getting recognized. I felt like I could get attention by acting out and that then maybe somebody would listen to me. That's when I went out of control."[7]

Kutcher (pictured in 2001) worked hard at being an excellent student until his senior year in high school when, frustrated with his life, he began to act out.

Ashton accumulated traffic citations while in high school. During his senior year, he also got caught for underage drinking. This violation had serious consequences, as it cost him the lead role in *Annie,* the school musical. He had been looking forward to playing Daddy Warbucks, but the incident took away that opportunity.

The punishment did not deter Ashton from further trouble, however. Later that year he rebelled again and with some other students broke into the high school. Years later he told an interviewer that he had intended to steal a test for his cousin, while another story quoted him as saying he had planned to take money from a soda machine. Regardless of his motivations, the break-in triggered the school's alarm, and the police arrived. Ashton telephoned his stepfather from jail, but Mark Portwood, who had once warned the teen that he would not bail him out if he got into trouble, refused to come and get him. Ashton spent the night in jail. He was released the next day and was later put on probation for his part in the crime.

College as a Second Choice

Ashton managed to get through high school without any other major incidents, and he graduated in 1996. In the fall he began classes at the University of Iowa in Iowa City, 20 miles (32km) from his hometown. Ashton's family could not afford to pay for his college education, so he took some unusual jobs in order to earn money for school. At various times he put shingles on roofs, sold his blood, and gutted and skinned deer. He also got a summer job at the General Mills plant in Cedar Rapids, where his father worked. His job was to vacuum up dust around the Cheerios line for twelve dollars an hour. "Can't beat that!" Ashton says. "Except I'd come home looking like a battered tenderloin."[8]

Although he still had thoughts of leaving Iowa to be an actor, Ashton displayed a practicality that has characterized much of his career. "I realized that unless I left for California, there wasn't anywhere for me to go with the acting," he says. "I couldn't afford to move that far, so I decided to go to school and become a genetic engineer."[9]

Factory workers at General Mills shovel wheat, raising clouds of dust. Kutcher worked at the plant one summer, vacuuming up dust.

In deciding to continue his education Ashton stayed true to one early goal, that of becoming a biochemical engineer. However, another dream lingered. And so, despite continued misgivings about fitting in, he realized he would need to stay in Iowa a while longer while he sorted out his ambitions.

Chapter 2

Fresh Face in Hollywood

College seemed like the right thing to do, but no matter how hard Kutcher tried, his heart was not in his schoolwork. He was torn between what he wanted to do and what he thought he should be doing, and his thoughts kept returning to acting.

Kutcher's freshman year was one of frustration and floundering. Nothing seemed to come easily to him at school, but everything changed one day in 1997, when an unexpected encounter with a talent scout took him away from Iowa and put his entertainment career in motion.

Life's a Party

Kutcher began college in the fall of 1996 with the intention of studying biochemical engineering, but he wasted a great deal of time that first semester. He drank, smoked marijuana, and neglected his studies. He sometimes woke up in the morning unable to remember what he had done the night before. "I played way too hard," he says, looking back. "I'm amazed I'm not dead." [10]

Kutcher's grades were poor, and he realized he needed to get his life back on track. He began to pay more attention to his classes, but he still was not happy with where his life appeared to be headed. Even when his academic performance improved, he felt out of place.

Conflicting feelings about his home state nagged at Kutcher. Though never wavering in his devotion to those close to him, he saw the general midwestern mindset as too narrow. He thought people were too comfortable with things as they were and did not question the status quo often enough. "I love the people that raised me and the people I was surrounded by," he said years later. "I love my whole family. But I think people need to ask questions—that's all I'm saying. The more questions you ask, the better off you'll be."[11] Kutcher again grew restless and thought more and more about a future away from Iowa.

Differing Goals

Kutcher continued to consider an acting career but had no interest in community theater or college productions. He felt Hollywood was the best place for him to pursue his dream, but

The old Iowa state capitol sits on the campus of the University of Iowa in Iowa City, where Kutcher enrolled as a biochemical engineering student in 1996.

Students relax in front of a television in their college dormitory. Kutcher had trouble studying with all of the distractions in his dorm.

the practical side of his nature told him that getting there would not be easy. "I wanted to come to Hollywood," he says. "But in Iowa it's like, 'How will I ever do that?'"[12]

As Kutcher considered his future, he began to question his commitment to his schoolwork. Some classes, particularly calculus, were difficult for him. It was not always easy for him to study in a noisy college dorm. In the middle of studying for a final exam for one of his freshman classes, he decided he had had enough. He wanted to be an actor, and he impulsively decided to take action on his dream.

Almost Out

Determined to use eight hundred dollars of his student loan to buy an airplane ticket to Hollywood, Kutcher called his sister and asked her to drive him to the airport. Tausha refused, and he was too afraid to ask anyone else for fear of being laughed at. Still intent on leaving Iowa, he decided to walk to the Cedar Rapids airport.

Kutcher packed a duffel bag, left his dorm room at 1 A.M., and began walking toward the airport. Five hours later he saw the sun peeking over the horizon. He was about halfway to the airport when his thoughts turned from determination to defeat. He began to think he was an idiot for believing he could pull off such a crazy idea. Then, just as suddenly as he had put down the books he'd been studying, Kutcher hid his duffel bag in a bush and walked to his mother's house. She drove him back to school and he got an A on the test he had been studying for. Kutcher passed all his classes in what was to be his final semester at the University of Iowa, although he got a D in calculus, and for a time he thought he would never become an actor.

What might have happened if Kutcher had succeeded in leaving Iowa that night? Years later he realized that wondering was beside the point, since success had come to him anyway. Although he had to wait a little longer for his acting career to begin, he felt that in the end everything worked out for the best. "It all happened how it needed to happen,"[13] he says.

Model Competitor

Instead of taking off with a sudden trip to Hollywood, Kutcher's career began with a chance meeting with a talent scout who spotted him in a Cedar Rapids bar. With his olive complexion, deep, dark eyes, and pouty lips, Kutcher caught the scout's eye as a good candidate for a state modeling competition.

When the talent scout approached Kutcher about entering a contest called the Fresh Face of Iowa, Kutcher was skeptical. When he thought of people who worked as models, he thought of women. Because he was not aware that "professional model" was a job description for men, he suspected the contest was some sort of a scam.

After he looked into the contest further, however, he found that it was legitimate. It dawned on him that the men he saw in advertisements were working as models, just as the women in the ads were. "I thought Fabio was the only male model," he says. "Then I realized, Oh, the 'Marlboro Man' isn't really a cowboy."[14]

Fresh Face of Iowa

That spring Kutcher entered the contest looking for 1997's Fresh Face of Iowa, and came away the winner. A modeling career progressed quickly. Within a few months agents were flying to Cedar Rapids to talk to him. In July the woman who had spotted him in the Cedar Rapids bar took him to New York to meet with more agents. After two days there, he signed with an agent and phoned his parents. He told them he was not coming back. Kutcher realized that he could not continue to be a student at the University

A sexy ad adorns this Abercrombie & Fitch store. Kutcher gained fame modeling for the company as well as for big-name fashion designers.

of Iowa and work as a model in New York. He chose modeling, and began using his middle name instead of his first name, to set himself apart from others in the business.

Work quickly came his way now that Kutcher was represented by the modeling agency Next. A week after signing with the agency he was modeling for Abercrombie and Fitch advertisements. Modeling jobs for Gucci, Versace, and Calvin Klein also came his way.

Kutcher's face appeared in magazine advertisements, and he also did runway shows in Milan and Paris. He could not believe how easy the work was. "All I had to do," he says, "was walk from here to the door and back." [15]

Angling Toward Acting

Although modeling was not a career Kutcher had ever intended to pursue, his assignments in the world of fashion were teaching him how to present himself in front of a camera. "I never set out to be a model, but it was a way into the business, so I ran with it," he says. "You learn a lot about how to hold yourself, and you get used to the camera, two skills that come in handy as an actor." [16] He realized that each modeling job was edging him closer to the acting career he dreamed of.

About eight months after he began modeling, Kutcher had an opportunity to act upon his ultimate dream. Auditions were being held in Los Angeles for a number of television shows, and he was invited to try out. His career as a model would be put on hold.

A Fantastic Day

Kutcher had a fantastic first day in Hollywood, and later recalled his experience with a mixture of amazement and modesty. "It was my first day in L.A. It was pretty exciting," he told writer Elizabeth Weltzman for *Interview* magazine. "I don't mess around." Then he laughed. "I say that like I had anything to do with it." [17]

Los Angeles and Hollywood can be a tough place for aspiring new actors, but Kutcher hit the big time on virtually his first day there.

On a single day in 1998, Kutcher was asked to audition for several shows. First he tried out for a comedy. He found out right away that he was not right for the part, but when a stranger approached him and asked him to also audition for another show, Kutcher quickly agreed.

The second audition meant a chance at a part in a planned series of hour-long episodes about the adventures of professional surfers. The show was called *Wind on Water* and starred Bo Derek. Kutcher was offered the part he tested for, but once he read the entire script he was not sure he wanted it. The concept behind the show did not make sense to him. Before agreeing to take the role, he decided to make sure there was nothing better available for him.

Kutcher had one more audition scheduled that day, for a situation comedy with the working title *Teenage Wasteland*. The physical setting was a small Wisconsin town, the time was 1976 (two years before Kutcher's birth), and the stories revolved around a group of close

Kelso-esque Characteristics

Kutcher finds both similarities and differences between himself and Kelso, the character he portrayed on *That '70s Show.* "I'm not as thickheaded or naïve as he is, but we have the same energy," Kutcher says. "He can't sit still. I'm like that. I always want to be on the go. If not breathing would save time for something more exciting, I'd give it up."

He says he tried to model Kelso after other dim but lovable television characters, Woody Harrelson in *Cheers* and John Travolta's character, Vinnie Barbarino, in *Welcome Back, Kotter.* He admits that when he first came to Hollywood he was as out of touch as Kelso was when it came to the entertainment business, but adds that the similarity was only short-lived. "When I first came to Los Angeles, I was a lot like my character because I was naïve to the way everything worked," he says. "Now I think we just look a lot alike."

Quoted in Carrie Bell, "Smooth Dude," *Teen Vogue,* Spring 2001, p. 106; and David Keeps, "The 25 Hottest Stars Under 25," *Teen People,* June 1, 2002, p. 99.

Kutcher played Michael Kelso (left) as a dim-witted but likeable character.

friends. Kutcher auditioned for the character of Michael Kelso, a dim-witted but likable friend of the main character.

Although he had limited acting experience, Kutcher's enthusiasm and innocence impressed Terry Turner, one of the show's creators. Cocreator Bonnie Turner was attracted to Kutcher because of his good looks and the way he played the character. "He got the role because everyone else was reading the character as stupid," Bonnie Turner says, "but Ashton made him naive."[18]

Timing and Instincts

Playing humorous roles seems to come naturally to Kutcher. He believes the secret to pulling them off is to not try to be funny and to get the timing down. "As soon as you're trying, it's not going to work," Kutcher says. "And I learned timing: It's like a waltz—one two three, one two three, setup setup punch line, setup setup punch line."[19]

On his first day in Hollywood, Kutcher was offered a part in the teen series, and he now had a choice to make. Still leery of the idea of a show about renegade surfers, Kutcher opted to go with the more down-to-earth concept of midwestern teenage buddies. His instincts were correct: *Wind on Water* was canceled after only a few episodes aired, but *That '70s Show*, as *Teenage Wasteland* was retitled, became the nation's top-rated show the week it premiered on the Fox network in 1998.

Critics did not rave about the show at first, with reviewer James Collins calling it "a typical teen comedy, only with '70s artifacts pasted into it." There was something appealing about the actors in the show, however, and Collins added, "Satirizing smiley faces and leisure suits is hardly fresh, although there's a sweetness and likability to the cast."[20]

Naïve About Hollywood?

Kutcher realized that his good fortune at the auditions had more to do with luck, his good looks, and his enthusiasm than with his acting talent. However, while he lacked professional acting experience, he did show the ability to make good business decisions. When confronted with a choice between two shows, he selected the one he felt was the more practical of the two, guessing that it stood the better chance of success.

Although he was at the very beginning of his career as an actor, Kutcher was already showing the uncanny business sense that would help him succeed. When choosing between the two series, he was not swayed by the prestige of working with established star Bo Derek. His instincts told him the surfer concept would not work, and he followed his intuition. Kutcher's practical side was at work here, and he was wise enough not to let his common sense be overshadowed by the glamour of Hollywood.

Yet despite his good business sense, Kutcher had arrived in California knowing very little about how a television series comes to be. He later commented that he had not known that a "pilot show" is a demonstration episode shown to producers before a series is chosen to air. He also said he did not realize shows got

Missing Millionaire

Kutcher almost had a chance to show off his intellect on the show *Who Wants to Be a Millionaire?* He was scheduled to appear on a celebrity version of the show with host Regis Philbin, with the stipulation that the show not air opposite *That '70s Show,* which was on another network. However, the day before Kutcher was to tape the show, the Fox network decided that it would not let him appear. To make up for Kutcher missing the show—and the potential to raise money for his favorite charity—Fox announced that it would donate $32,000 to the University of Iowa's support center for families of transplant patients. Kutcher had planned to give his prize money to the center because of his brother Michael's transplant surgery.

canceled: "All the shows that I watched—*The Cosby Show, Roseanne* and *Diff'rent Strokes*—were on for years."[21]

Kutcher may not have known much about the details of show business, but he was able to get work quickly, which is unusual for novice actors. He soon had a new agent, Stephanie Simon, who was impressed by Kutcher's self-assurance and was happy to help him take care of business details such as contracts.

For a young man who a year earlier had been an unhappy college student, Kutcher's fortunes were looking up. After desperately wanting to leave his home state but seeing no way out, Kutcher had traveled the world and landed his dream job. Although he was playing the part of a dim-witted character, Kutcher was anything but. A quick learner, he was capable of making practical business decisions. His career had something else in its favor: his natural instinct for comic timing. That, coupled with his good looks and drive to succeed, soon began attracting attention.

Chapter 3

Making Dimness Pay

Kutcher snagged his first acting role soon after arriving in California, and he spent his first years in Hollywood playing likable, funny, dim-witted characters. However, it was not long before people learned that he was anything but dim in real life. Those judging him by his appearance were soon surprised by the depth of his intellect.

Kutcher's intelligence came through in conversations with his costars, and his work ethic impressed directors. However, onscreen he continued to play characters known for their good looks rather than their brains. He had some opportunities to experiment with small roles that were outside the realm of the goofy Kelso he played so well on *That '70s Show,* but these ventures were not very successful. Kutcher was nevertheless broadening his horizons in the entertainment business, eagerly learning more about what went on behind the scenes in particular. As he looked into producing shows, he was discovering what would sell.

That '70s Star Impresses His Peers

As Kelso, the spacey, good-looking, long-haired teen, Kutcher soon became one of the most recognizable faces of *That '70s Show. Interview* magazine called Kelso a mixture of the naïve '60s sitcom character Gomer Pyle and '70s teen idol Shaun Cassidy. Despite critics' reservations, the show was a hit, and by the end of 1998 Kutcher was gaining national attention. In a feature article, *People* reported on Kutcher's rapid rise from Homestead to Hollywood. The article also discussed the adjustments the actor, who had grown up during the '80s and '90s, had to make in order to play a teen in the '70s.

He may have been new in town, but Kutcher was making an impression on the rest of the cast of *That '70s Show*. "We found out how smart he was when we were sitting around talking about high-school science," says Danny Masterson, who played Kelso's friend Steven Hyde on the show. "He started rattling off stuff about chemicals and the body."[22]

Mila Kunis, the fourteen-year-old actress who played Kelso's girlfriend, Jackie, offered Kutcher a different type of compliment—more in keeping with the general opinion of teen girls. "He's got very nice lips," she said. "He's also got nice deep eyes, nice bone structure and a toned body. He's a hottie."[23]

Kelso (standing) talks with friends in a scene from That '70s Show. *Kutcher was one of the show's most recognizable faces.*

Cool History Lesson

When he began memorizing dialogue for *That '70s Show,* Kutcher was a bit surprised by the vocabulary. He did not know that the word "cool" had been popular then; he thought it belonged to his generation. "You know, we're saying 'cool' all the time on the show," he says. "I didn't think 'cool' was around then. It ticks me off. You think your generation came up with a word, and we didn't!"

The show also taught him a bit about the people behind the music from that era. "There was all this music from the '70s that I had heard but never knew who did it," he says, "like the Captain and Tennille."

Quoted in *People,* "Spirit of '76," November 2, 1998, p. 75.

Kunis also appreciated Kutcher in a professional way, however, and applauded his attitude on the set. Half a dozen years younger than her costar, she had been nervous about the kissing scenes she knew they would have, but she noted that he made her feel comfortable with these scenes by making jokes about them.

Free Time

Kutcher's costars on the show also became his close friends. Wilmer Valderrama, who played a foreign exchange student named Fez, and Masterson joked around with Kutcher on the set, and when the three actors were not working they saw each other socially. "When we started the show, we were all pretty new to the city and the business, so we clung to each other," Kutcher says. "We've become like a family."[24]

Off the set, Kutcher liked spending time with his friends and at home, downloading music from the Internet, watching football, and playing basketball. He was thrilled to finally be making enough money to buy the things he needed, but he did not live extravagantly. After being in Los Angeles for three months, Kutcher was earning enough money to afford a spacious two-bedroom apartment in West Hollywood. He later purchased a new home and a car, the first one he owned that wasn't more than a decade old.

Model Relationship

Kutcher also spent time with his girlfriend, model January Jones. They had met in 1998 during a photo shoot for the Abercrombie and Fitch catalog, one of his first modeling assignments. They struck up a friendship, and began dating the next year.

The dating relationship, which stemmed from the friendship, was not perfect. The couple tried to work things out when they disagreed, however. "Even if we get in a fight, we'll hate each other for a day, but then the next day, we fall in love all over again,"[25] Kutcher said.

Movie Roles

In addition to his ongoing part in *That '70s Show,* Kutcher also landed small film roles. In the 1999 comedy *Coming Soon,* he played a character known only by his first name, Louie. In the action movie *Reindeer Games,* which was released in 2000 and starred Ben Affleck, he played an unnamed college student. In the romantic comedy *Down to You,* which starred Freddie Prinze Jr. and Julia Stiles and was also released in 2000, Kutcher was cast as a character with a well-known name. He played a character named Jim Morrison, who patterned his life after that of the lead singer of the '60s rock band the Doors. These parts generated little screen time for Kutcher, but they were small steps in taking his career from television to the big screen.

Kutcher's first larger movie role was in *Texas Rangers,* which was filmed in the summer of 1999 between the first two seasons of *That '70s Show.* The Western, set in the years immediately following the Civil War, starred James Van Der Beek, Dylan McDermott, and Rachel Leigh Cook. For this role Kutcher had to learn some horsemanship, and was also called upon to shoot a pistol and shotgun simultaneously. He was happy to play a cowboy, saying it reminded him of the movies he enjoyed watching as a child. "I grew up watching John Wayne movies with my grandfather," he says. "He'll only watch Westerns, and I really wanted to make a movie my grandpa would see."[26]

While Kutcher was excited about making the movie, he had to wait patiently for it to be released to the public. The movie was handicapped by a poor script, and the studio was reluctant to place it in theaters. The original release date was August 2000,

Kutcher poses at the premiere of Down to You *with costars Julia Stiles (center) and Selma Blair in 2000. He had roles in three films that year.*

but *Entertainment Weekly* noted that the film's lack of quality and authenticity delayed its release until April 2001. That spring the studio decided on a second postponement, and in November 2001 the movie was finally released.

Although the movie was not highly regarded, Kutcher's reputation was enhanced while he was making it. Not for the first time, his high energy level and strong work ethic were noticed on the set. "Ashton is like a puppy," says Steve Miner, the director of *Texas Rangers,* who had also directed *Wild Hearts Can't Be Broken* and the horror movies *Halloween: H₂0* and *Friday the 13th Part 2.* "He just doesn't stop. He worked hard at riding and shooting and all the cowboy stuff. I wanted to hook up a cable to him and harness some of his energy—it would save on generator costs."[27]

Awestruck by Success

Kutcher's energy was fueling a rapidly rising career. In March 2000 *Seventeen* magazine profiled him as one of six promising young actors, and in May 2000 he was named one of *People* magazine's 50 Most Beautiful People in the World. The good looks that had helped him win the modeling competition were also attracting attention in Hollywood.

At age twenty-two, Kutcher was awed by how quickly he had achieved success in Hollywood. Just a few years earlier, he would not have thought it was within his reach. "I walk through my house that I shouldn't have and get in my car that I shouldn't have and go to my job that I shouldn't have and believe that I'm the luckiest guy in the world,"[28] he said.

Kutcher did not try to pretend that he was a highly trained actor. He credited his performances to instinct. His looks and comic timing set him apart—as well as, he jokingly added, a distinctive haircut. "When you do comedy, there's a certain instinct that you need to have," he says. "I try to do it differently than anybody else. And I have funny-looking legs, so I can usually make people laugh by showing them off. Plus, I'm one of the only younger actors with a '70s haircut. Beat that!"[29]

That '70s Hair

As one of the stars of *That '70s Show,* Kutcher had to look like a teen from that era. He could take off the bell-bottoms and polyester shirts when he was away from the set, but he had to keep his long '70s hairstyle, which sometimes frustrated him. "The problem with long hair is that I have to fuss with it," he said. "I hate to mess with it." To tame his hair, he did as little with it as possible. In the morning, he simply wet it and shook it. He advised people with a similar hairstyle to wash their hair no more than weekly. "Never condition your hair—it makes it fluffy and nasty," he said. "I wash my hair once a week, and look at it."

Quoted in *People,* "Ashton Kutcher: Actor," May 8, 2000, p. 161; and Deanna Kizis, "Ashton Kutcher on Past Party Days and His Rock-Solid Relationship," *Cosmopolitan,* February 2001, p. 174.

Dude!

Kutcher built on his reputation as a comic actor with his next movie, *Dude, Where's My Car?* Filmed in the summer of 2000, the movie featured Kutcher as Montgomery II, a character not too far removed from Kelso in *That '70s Show.* Seann William Scott, a veteran of teen films such as *American Pie* and *Road Trip,* played his buddy Chester Greenburg, and the plot hinged on the pair's inability to remember what happened to their car after a wild night of partying.

The comedy, directed by Danny Leiner, was aimed at teens and included a heavy dose of goofy humor. It lacked deep meaning and intellectual challenges. Upon the release of the lighthearted feature in December 2000, *Variety* reviewer Joe Leydon said it appeared to have been "made by the proudest underachievers this side of Bart Simpson. Pic is transparently thin—even at just 83 minutes it feels desperately padded—but fitfully amusing." [30]

While Leydon noted that *Dude* was not a quality movie, he rightly predicted that it would do well with its teenaged target audience because there were no other comparable movies around at the time. *Dude* was an enjoyable diversion for teens looking for a movie to see during winter break, and it developed a following among high school and college students.

In Character

Kutcher's personality is much edgier and sharper than the mellow character he played in *Dude,* but the actor admits that when he was a teenager there were similarities between himself and Jesse. He also partied too much, beginning to drink in high school, and, in college, smoking marijuana. There were times when he could not remember what be had done the night before. At that

Kutcher and costar Seann William Scott arrive at the premiere of Dude, Where's My Car? *in the jalopy used in the film. The movie became a teen cult flick.*

stage in his life, he did not think much about listening to what others had to say. "I thought I knew everything but I didn't have a clue,"[31] he says.

Although in *Dude* Kutcher played basically the same character he portrayed on television, his reputation as an actor was boosted by the movie. His characterization of Jesse was light and engaging. Leydon noted that "Kutcher plays Jesse with a touch of sweetness and a hint of vulnerability, which serves the character well."[32]

Cashing In

Kutcher realized that *Dude* would win no Academy Awards, but he saw his role of Jesse as a good career move. The movie showed that he had the power to capture a teen audience in theaters as well as on television. Kutcher admitted that the movie would never be confused with one of Shakespeare's plays, but added that two of his favorite movies were the simplistic comedies *Dumb and Dumber* and *Tommy Boy*.

When a reporter asked him if he had ever compromised his career and made a movie just for the money, he said he had not. He defended his decisions, saying that making a movie with a big studio could be just as satisfying as making a more artistic niche movie with a smaller studio. His goal was to develop a career that had staying power, and he did not see it as a mistake to take the occasional entertaining, if mindless, role. His long-term plans, however, involved more significant fare. He noted that he wanted to be an actor in the mold of Tom Cruise, making movies for years.

Celebrity Pressures

Kutcher was becoming a recognizable face, mainly among teens and preteens who liked *That '70s Show* and admired his good

Kutcher takes a moment to greet fans at an MTV live show. Thrilled with the recognition at first, his fame later became a burden.

looks. It was sometimes reassuring to the young actor to be recognized in public, as that told him that he had reached a certain level of stardom. Such was the case while he was doing an interview in the spring of 2001 with a reporter in a Los Angeles coffeehouse. Two preteens shyly asked him for an autograph after spying on him for an hour. A fourteen-year-old sitting nearby was too shy to approach him, and could only stare. "I'm not sure why anyone would be afraid of me," he says. "I guess when I was a kid, seeing a celebrity would have been a big deal. Maybe I'd have been shy too. . . . Some days that recognition is the best thing that can happen to you. It means you're doing something right." [33]

Recognition was not always a good thing for Kutcher. He also began encountering the difficulties that came with being a celebrity. He became friends with the members of the pop group Hanson, which was composed of three brothers, after they did a television show together. He went to see one of the group's concerts, but at the event Kutcher's fans recognized him and he was mobbed as he tried to get to his seat. "I've never seen anything like it . . . those girls literally took my girlfriend and threw her out of the way," he says. "It was one of the scariest moments of my life." [34]

While young people liked Kutcher, he did not feel the same support for his relationship with Jones. His fans would have liked to see him single. "When you're in a relationship, everybody wants you to break up," he says. "People hate seeing you happy when they're not." [35] Although *Cosmopolitan* magazine used the term "rock solid" to describe the relationship in the headline of a February 2001 article, Kutcher and Jones broke up later that year.

Teen Idol with a Plan

For better and worse, Kutcher had become a teen idol thanks to his fresh face and model's good looks. He did not see anything wrong with taking advantage of the attention that came with his looks, and using it to bring teens to his show and movies. He did not want to be stereotyped into that type of role, however, or have a stint as a teen idol be the high point of his career.

In order to broaden his roles and his career, Kutcher had to think beyond the goofy characters for which he was best known. "I don't think there's anything wrong with being pushed to attract a younger audience," he said. "But you're not always going to be able to play a teen. So you do have to step away eventually and find your place in a different category." [36]

Kutcher had played his dim-witted characters in *Dude* and *That '70s Show* so well that he began to be associated with them, in spite of the more thoughtful and intelligent side he showed to his costars and reporters. He departed from his usual role in *Texas Rangers,* but its delayed release, followed by poor reviews, did little to advance his reputation as a versatile actor. Kutcher would have to find another way to prove that his talents went beyond his good looks.

Kutcher's character in **Dude, Where's My Car** *(pictured) and that of Kelso in* **That '70s Show** *got him stereotyped as a dimwit.*

New Direction

In addition to trying to find different types of movie roles, Kutcher began looking at different avenues to make a living in the entertainment field. He realized that his acting ability might be limited, but knew that his talents went beyond acting. To further his career, he was determined to delve into the business side of Hollywood.

Kutcher did not limit himself to working in front of the camera. He also had ideas for television shows, and believed that by gaining experience as a producer he would have a fallback career if acting did not work out. His popularity among teens gave him some name recognition and he wanted to capitalize on it to gain access to studio executives who could help him turn his ideas into reality. He did not want to take his fame for granted, but instead use it to help him establish a solid career in entertainment. "The American dream is having a job you love, and I have never felt like I was watching the clock on the set, waiting to punch out," he says. "Making it in Hollywood is half luck and half talent, so I am always on my computer, writing, going to meetings, trying to learn all sides of the business."[37]

Chapter 4

Producer

By 2001 Kutcher was no longer a fresh face in Hollywood. He had achieved a degree of fame, but he could not count on getting work simply because of his looks. His career had taken off rapidly, and he did not want things to cool down.

As much as Kutcher loves acting, he has always tended to doubt that his talent would be sufficient to carry him to the top as an actor. To diversify, therefore, he looked for opportunities to be involved in other aspects of making movies and television programs, from writing to producing. Although some underestimated his ability, assuming him to be clueless and simpleminded like the characters he played, those who took time to speak with Kutcher came away impressed by his ideas and drive.

Moving Behind the Scenes

Kutcher had his first opportunity to do some work behind the scenes as well as in front of the camera in 2001 when he starred in a movie tentatively titled *The Guest,* playing a young man whose boss asks him to house-sit. Kutcher's character agrees, motivated by the desire to get closer to the boss's good-looking daughter, played by Tara Reid.

The movie marked a turning point in Kutcher's career. For the first time, he had an interest in a movie beyond acting in it. He was a coproducer on the project, which also had an executive producer, an associate producer, and two other producers. Although he was far from the only person with input into the project, Kutcher put a dedicated effort into multiple aspects of

Tara Reid costarred with Kutcher in **My Boss's Daughter,** *which was also Kutcher's producing debut.*

the movie's production. "I'm kind of a control freak, so for *The Guest* I put a lot of time into reworking it and helping with casting,"[38] Kutcher says.

Kutcher's efforts notwithstanding, the final product did not turn out well. It was shelved for two years before it was released, under the new title *My Boss's Daughter.* The reviews were awful, and Kutcher did nothing to publicize the release. During production, however, he impressed his costar, who predicted big things for him. "There's something about Ashton—he just shines," says Tara Reid. "He's charming, sweet, a great actor. You know he's going to be a big star. He just has that magnetic quality." [39]

Punk'd

It did not take Kutcher long to find another project to produce. In the summer of 2002 he pitched an idea for a television show, initially called *Harassment.* The idea was for Kutcher to play pranks on his unsuspecting celebrity friends and show their reactions, a premise that came from the old television show *Candid Camera.* "Originally, I wanted to create a new platform for young comedians because the only thing out there for them to show their stuff on was a showcase, or they could try to get on *Saturday Night Live,*" he says. "I decided to start pulling practical jokes on my friends, and then, of course, the network really liked the fact that some of my friends were celebrities." [40]

The practical jokes were designed to garner emotional responses from the celebrities, revealing a raw side of their personalities not often seen by the public. By catching the rich and famous at unguarded moments, the program would show how ordinary celebrities could be.

The concept for the show was a product of Kutcher's feelings toward his colleagues in Hollywood. Although he was one of the hottest young stars in the entertainment industry, Kutcher was sometimes uncomfortable among the celebrity set. He had risen to fame in only a few years, and for all his involvement in movies and television, he still felt like an outsider who watched as other famous people went about their lives. In shooting episodes of *Punk'd* he was able to see celebrities at their most human. Showing this side of the celebrities on television, he believed, would be good for both the public and the celebrities. "I think what's fun about it is that people get to see a celebrity doing just what they do on a regular basis and then reacting to a situation just like anyone else would—which is kind of great," he says. "And for the celebrities, it forces them to look at themselves for a second and go, 'Wow, I'm really trying to use my fame to my advantage,' so I think that's a good thing."[41]

Planning a Punking

The reality show was picked up by MTV and given the new title *Punk'd*. In order to make the practical jokes work, Kutcher had to do some elaborate planning. He and a friend, Jason Goldberg, would decide on each show's target, study the person's habits, and select an appropriate prank. Kutcher would then develop the concept of the prank in enough detail to allow others to write a script for the actors who would draw the celebrity into the faked situation.

Pulling the pranks also involved taking care of a number of production details. Kutcher and his staff had to choose a location, get any necessary props, and find or make places to hide cameras. They also had to acquire any necessary permits from local authorities, make sure that everything connected with the activity about to be staged was legal, and talk their plan over with the proposed target's managers and publicists. Kutcher had to know the intended subject of the punking well, to give him a sense of how far the person could be pushed. He did not want to cause emotional distress, for obvious reasons. "Everyone will lose it at a certain point," Kutcher said. "But we're not out to cause harm. We have to be constantly aware of a person's feelings, so as not to cross the line."[42]

When the show debuted in 2003, singer Justin Timberlake was one of the first celebrities to be put on the spot. Kutcher sent a crew to Timberlake's home, supposedly to repossess the pop star's cars and other valuables. Timberlake was near tears when he thought his things were being taken away, but when Kutcher appeared and revealed the prank he laughed about it— and then resumed his status as a star, ordering everyone to leave his property.

A Perfectionist

Kutcher watched each practical joke unfold from television monitors in a van near the location of the prank. Hidden cameras captured the reaction of the famous subject, and other cameras in the van recorded Kutcher's reaction to the situation. The tapes were edited, and Kutcher later added commentary to underscore his view of how the joke went.

Oscar winner Halle Berry laughs with Kutcher after he reveals that she has just been punk'd.

It soon became clear that Kutcher was a perfectionist. His reputation was at stake, and he did not want an episode to fall through because of poor planning or incompetence. When an earpiece stopped working at one point during a punking he became upset. His friend and coworker Goldberg vouches for his determined attitude. "His work ethic is sickening, it's out of control,"[43] Goldberg says.

A Hit

Kutcher's perfectionistic efforts were well spent, as the show became a success. The combination of celebrity guests and their humbled expressions struck a chord with viewers, and Kutcher's comments about the practical jokes proved to be entertaining rather than gloating. "It's more fun than most hidden-camera shows: Kutcher keeps his in-your-face energy from boiling over into obnoxiousness," wrote reviewers Tom Gliatto and Frank Swertlow in *People*.

Punking the Audience

In December 2003 Kutcher announced that his MTV show *Punk'd* was finished after two seasons. "We have had an incredible time doing the show and have decided to stick with the old adage of 'leave 'em wanting more,' and that's how we feel with the show," Kutcher says.

Not everyone believed the show would actually go off the air, however, as ratings were still high. The following April that speculation proved to be correct when it was announced that the joke had been on the audience and *Punk'd* would be back for a third season of pranks.

Quoted in Denise Martin, "Kutcher Unplugs 'Punk'd,'" *Daily Variety,* December 15, 2003, p. 30.

Kutcher shares the podium with Jessica Simpson at the 2001 Teen Choice Awards.

"And there are worse ways to waste half an hour than watching stars being humiliated."[44]

Kutcher and his crew were creative in their jokes. In one prank, people pretending to be relatives of Jessica Simpson parked a vehicle outside the home Simpson shared with then-husband Nick Lachey, demanding that Lachey give them five thousand dollars to leave. In another, they convinced Frankie Muniz that a valet had taken his new Porsche. The singer Pink was fooled into believing her boyfriend had been arrested for stealing motorbikes.

Punk'd succeeded because it managed to make fun of people without being cruel. The joke was on the celebrities, but when it was over and they realized they had been set up, they were able to laugh at themselves. "*Punk'd* is a subversive slice of comic hilarity,"[45] wrote reviewer Michael Endelman in *Entertainment Weekly*.

More than Pulling Pranks

The magazine reviewer added that the show was an intriguing look at how stars act, showing Kelly Osbourne swearing at her mother and Stephen Dorff walking out on a check. Taking away the benefits of fame that celebrities have come to expect created an uncomfortable situation for some, but that was Kutcher's intention. "Take that away, it becomes a very raw place for people," Kutcher says. "But it also gives them value in the things that count. Because if you lose your house and your money and everything there is, what are you left with? Yourself. And the people who love you. It sounds corny, but there is that lesson."[46]

Kutcher was not shy about showing the unflattering side of a celebrity's personality, as he wanted his show to make a statement about human nature. He hoped it made people look more closely at themselves and their reactions to the world around them. The premise worked, and MTV liked the show so much that two more seasons were ordered in the summer of 2003.

Avoiding a Punking

Playing tricks on friends such as Justin Timberlake and costars such as Wilmer Valderamma made Kutcher a likely target for revenge. However, he was so used to setting up practical jokes that he was difficult to trick. While he admitted that little things such as a coffee shop not being open when he expected it to be could throw him off, he hoped that in a true emergency he would be more concerned about others than about himself. He knew that the key to not getting punk'd was to not overreact to any situation, so he doubted that anyone who was able to trick him would get a shockingly out-of-character response.

Lost Episode

Not everyone was a good sport about being the subject of one of Kutcher's practical jokes on his show *Punk'd*. When an actor posing as a waiter began harassing baseball player Alex Rodriguez as he had dinner with his wife in a Los Angeles restaurant, the situation became heated. The "waiter" provoked the New York Yankees third baseman by saying he was a loser whose teams had never been winners. After the joke was revealed, Rodriguez refused to sign a release form and the tape from the show was destroyed.

Continuing in Comedy

His *Punk'd* producing venture was going well, but Kutcher did not stop being an actor. He still enjoyed working in front of the camera, continuing to work on *That '70s Show* and making the movie *Just Married,* a farce about a young couple on their honeymoon.

In *Just Married,* Kutcher played Tom, a young sports fan recently wed to the rich, worldly Sarah, played by Brittany Murphy. On their European honeymoon, the dissimilarities in their personalities become apparent. The movie derives its humor from their different preferences, with Tom opting to sit in a sports bar in Venice rather than visit a church or museum, and slapstick situations such as Kutcher's character cramming his long legs into a tiny rental car.

The couple argues constantly onscreen, and the actors' relationship also got off to a rocky start on the set. "We had this big blowout fight," Kutcher recalls. "She hated me. I hated her. It was a straight-up argument. But we both apologized to each other later."[47]

Filming went well after that, and Murphy later laughed about the incident, saying she could not remember what it had been about. Murphy was considered a capable film actress; she had appeared in *Clueless* and had played Eminem's girlfriend in *8 Mile*. However, neither she nor Kutcher received good reviews for *Just Married*. Owen Gleiberman called the movie "lively dumb fun" and criticized the script, saying, "*Just Married* collapses into the most generic sort of teen movie-ville just at the moment it's con-

British tabloid models flank Kutcher at the 2003 London opening of his movie Just Married.

Kutcher and then-girlfriend Ashley Scott oblige the paparazzi at a 2001 movie premiere. The couple split up in 2002.

vinced you that its lightly appealing stars are capable of better."[48] The movie pulled in an average audience at the box office, but Kutcher was having more success as a producer than an actor.

Brittany Murphy

The so-so performance of *Just Married* had little effect on Kutcher professionally, but the film made a big impact on his personal life. Kutcher and his costar became a real-life couple several months after the movie's production ended in mid-2002. While they were making the movie, Kutcher was wrapping up a relationship with actress Ashley Scott, and Murphy was still stinging from a recent breakup. "I had a broken heart when we first met, and he was in a very serious relationship with a lovely young woman, but we just clicked and had a great time filming," she says. "Then I went away to do a film, he went away to do a film, and it was about [November 2002] when we looked at each other and thought, 'OK, this is something.'" [49]

Once Kutcher and Murphy found time to get to know each other, they got along very well indeed, with Kutcher telling a *Cosmopolitan* interviewer that they "were idiots not to be spending time together." [50]

After a few public appearances together, however, Kutcher pulled back from the relationship. In the interview in *Cosmopolitan* magazine, he hesitated to say that he and Murphy were a couple, suggesting that he preferred to be with her because he wanted to, not because she was his girlfriend and he had to. "I really feel that when you're dating someone your expectations go way up, and all of a sudden you can't do this and you can't do that," he says. "If you treat the other person with kindness just because you want to, there's no red tape." [51] The relationship with Murphy did not last much longer, and they broke up after seven months together.

Dreaming Bigger

Kutcher was becoming an increasingly popular star, and was traveling in some powerful celebrity circles. He met Sean "P. Diddy" Combs at an NBA All-Star game and quickly hit it off with the rapper and producer. He also told a writer for *Rolling Stone* that President George W. Bush's daughters, Jenna and Barbara, had been to a party at his house.

While Kutcher was often surrounded by other celebrities when he went to movie premieres and parties, he was still new enough to Hollywood to feel amazed by the level of fame he had attained. When he and some friends drove by the 20th Century Fox studio lot and saw that it had a *Just Married* billboard in front of it, they stopped to take a picture. Kutcher couldn't help looking at the billboard and being awed by all that had happened to him in a short period of time. "I feel like I don't know how much of this is real," he says. "It's the most bizarre thing in the world

The Real Thing

When Kutcher was dating Brittany Murphy, an interviewer asked him if it was weird to kiss Brittany in the movie and then kiss her for real. Kutcher said that movie kisses are completely different than real kisses. On a movie, there's so much going on and so many other things to think about that there is no time for passion. "During the movie, I was always busy thinking, 'What's my next line?'" he says. "But when I kissed her for the first time for real, it was a whole new experience. I was like 'Oh my God! You have the best lips I have ever kissed in my life.'"

Quoted in Deanna Kizis, "Ashton Kutcher on Past Party Days and His Rock-Solid Relationship," *Cosmopolitan,* February 2001, p. 174.

Lovebirds Kutcher and Murphy attended the 2003 NBA All-Star Game.

when your dreams become reality. You just don't know how to react." [52]

Kutcher's contemplations in front of the billboard were interrupted when a girl pulled up in a car, looked at him and the billboard, and began laughing at his expression. No one expected a celebrity to look bemused by his own fame. Although he could scarcely believe what he had already accomplished, Kutcher was still not satisfied. He wanted something more and felt he needed a plan for the rest of his life.

To remind himself to press forward and not rest on his accomplishments, Kutcher taped a piece of paper reading "Dream Bigger" to his phone. He did not want to be content. For all he had done, something was still lacking, and he wanted to continue to find new ways to succeed.

Chapter 5

New Projects, New Relationship

K utcher's goal was to entertain people as well as teach them something about human nature. While he continued his role as the goofy Kelso on *That '70s Show,* he was also making a dramatic movie with a message. He continued to produce his reality show, but he was moving away from silly teen-oriented fare and toward projects that showed the more thoughtful side of his personality.

Changes were also occurring in Kutcher's personal life. At age twenty-five his face began appearing on the covers of more and more celebrity gossip magazines, but it was not because of his acting ability or savvy as a producer. In 2003 he began a relationship with actress Demi Moore, a woman fifteen years his senior. When they began dating, public interest in both of them intensified.

Meeting Demi

Soon after Kutcher broke up with Murphy, he met another woman, one who would make a huge impact on his life. At a casual group dinner in New York, a friend introduced him to Demi Moore. The pair soon became deeply engaged in conversation. At first Kutcher had no idea of Moore's background as an actress, but simply enjoyed talking with her. They talked for half an hour before he realized she was someone famous.

They eventually had to mingle with other guests, but Kutcher told Moore he had to talk to her later. She did not believe him at first, but

This entrance leads to the Los Angeles restaurant Dolce, which Kutcher partly owned. He and Demi Moore often dined there.

he was serious. After the dinner they went to her apartment and talked all night long. "You talk about meeting your soul mate," she said two years later. "I truly feel I have been given that gift."[53]

Interesting Couple

The pair continued to spend time together, and their relationship was of immediate interest to the press. Considerably more experienced than Kutcher, Moore had been acting since the early 1980s, and had been married twice, to rock musician Freddy Moore from 1980 to 1984 and to actor Bruce Willis from 1987 to 2000. She and Willis had three daughters, who were fourteen, eleven, and nine years old when Moore and Kutcher started dating.

Their relationship was also intriguing because it coincided with Moore's return to acting. She had taken a break from Hollywood to raise her three daughters away from the spotlight, and had been living in Idaho. When she and Kutcher began seeing each other, she had recently finished making *Charlie's Angels: Full Throttle,* her first movie in several years. Kutcher's reputation as a practical joker added another level of interest to their relationship. When Moore and Kutcher were together, people were not sure if they were seeing a budding romance or if Kutcher was setting up an elaborate prank on the public.

A Kiss Is Just a Kiss

Soon after they began dating, Kutcher brought Moore to the set of *Cheaper by the Dozen*, a remake of the 1950 classic starring Clifton Webb as the father of twelve. As a favor to director Shawn Levy, who had worked with Kutcher on *Just Married*, Kutcher took a small role in the movie as the boyfriend of the oldest daughter in the clan. However, on the day Moore came to the set he was scheduled to film a kissing scene with Piper Perabo, who played his girlfriend in the movie. When she met Moore, Perabo tried to ease the situation by saying, "Hi, you're gorgeous! I'll be kissing your boyfriend in about 10 minutes." Moore, herself a professional actress, accepted the greeting graciously and when the movie premiered in December 2003, she attended with Kutcher and her three daughters.

Quoted in Tom Cunneff, "Queen Bee," *People*, December 29, 2003, p. 47.

Demi Moore and daughters join Kutcher at Cheaper by the Dozen's *opening in 2003.*

Celebrity Sightings

As people wondered whether Kutcher and Moore really were a couple, their comings and goings were well chronicled by celebrity magazines. On April 30, 2003, they were spotted having dinner at a restaurant, and then going to a nightclub and dancing to hip-hop music. In mid-May they were seen together in a Los Angeles restaurant called Dolce, in which Kutcher was an investor. They then jetted to Miami and had dinner with Combs and his girlfriend, Kim Porter, and went on a cruise to the Bahamas.

Moore and Kutcher were not shy about their affection for one another. On May 31, 2003, *People* reported that Moore and Kutcher appeared together at the MTV Movie Awards in Hollywood. "They flirted with each other all night," an observer told a reporter for the magazine. "It looked like they were in that giddy phase, when you start to fall for someone."[54] After the awards ceremony they went to a party thrown by Combs at an estate in Benedict Canyon, and the next day they appeared together by the pool at the Beverly Hills Hotel.

Publicity Stunt

Because of all the press attention, some thought the romance between Kutcher and Moore was a publicity stunt. The summer after they met, she was promoting her first movie in years, leading some to suspect that her relationship with the much younger man was a bid for publicity. Kutcher's celebrity status had never been higher. He was given a number of Teen Choice Awards by *Teen People* magazine, and *People* named him America's hottest bachelor. "He is the hottest male star out there right now for the teen market," said *Teen People* editor Amy Barnett. "Anything he does right now is golden."[55]

It bothered Kutcher that anyone would think he was dating Moore to become a bigger celebrity. He had accomplished a great deal on his own and resented the implication that he was using Moore to draw attention to himself. "If people think that's why I'm doing well, it bothers me," Kutcher says. "Before I even met Demi, I managed to figure out how to be on a sitcom for five years, produce my own television show and make a couple of films that did extremely well." [56]

Like a Parent

When he began dating Moore, Kutcher took on another role as well. When he was with Moore and her daughters, he was like a parent to Rumer, Scout, and Tallulah. Rather than resenting the children as hindrances to the relationship, as some men his age might, he saw them as a great addition to it. He was comfortable with Moore's family from the start and counted himself fortunate to be part of the children's lives. "I feel like they've been shafted in the deal," he says. "I get four of them [including Moore] and all they get is me. They got the short end of the stick." [57]

Kutcher did not try to take the place of the girls' father, Bruce Willis, who was very involved in his daughters' lives.

Kutcher's relationship with Moore included going out with her three daughters and their father, action star Bruce Willis.

Willis, in turn, did not stand in the way of Moore's relationship with Kutcher and the younger man's involvement with their children. When Moore attended movie premieres with her daughters and Kutcher, Willis was also in attendance at times. At the Los Angeles premiere of *Charlie's Angels: Full Throttle*, Moore was accompanied by Kutcher, her children, and her ex-husband.

Moore's children were pleased to have Kutcher around as well. In fact, when Tallulah and Scout set up a lemonade stand, they advertised the venture with a sign saying that this was where Ashton Kutcher bought lemonade. After Moore moved her children to Los Angeles from Idaho, Kutcher sometimes took the girls to school or sports practices.

Split Personality

Kutcher seemed very much a family man when he was with Moore and her children, but he also continued to be seen with other Hollywood celebrities. He and Combs talked regularly, and he also continued to be friendly with his costars of *That '70s Show*. His life was changing as he balanced his relationship with Moore and her family with a star-studded celebrity lifestyle.

As he matured as a Hollywood celebrity, Kutcher sometimes exhibited a split personality. He could be silly one moment, businesslike the next. When doing an interview for a *TV Guide* story, he did an elaborate good-bye handshake with *That '70s Show* costar Valderrama, and then talked seriously about the profits others earned by taking his picture when he was in public. He sometimes wore hip-hop clothes, including a large necklace Combs had given him, and at other times dressed in a suit and tie.

As Kutcher's relationship with Moore deepened, he spent less time hanging out at clubs and seeking out celebrity pals. "Since they've been together, he has blossomed and has become a lot more responsible," [58] says Greg Link, who has been a friend of Kutcher's since his days as a model. Kutcher grew up as the

Ashton Kutcher's persona includes being silly, as at the 2000 VH-1 Music Awards, and being serious, as at this New York fashion show.

relationship turned more serious, and a new "Rat Pack" he and Combs discussed never materialized.

Serious Acting

Kutcher's career continued to mature as well. In 2003 he was a coproducer of *The Butterfly Effect*, in which he also had his first serious lead role as an actor. He played a man who tries to fix his past by traveling back in time, and experiences the sometimes odd and bizarre repercussions of his decisions. Kutcher saw the role as an opportunity to shake up people's expectations of him. "I just want to surprise people," he says. "I don't think people think I can handle a dramatic movie. So I want to be good. No, I want to be great." [59]

Because of his previous work as a comic actor and reality show host, Kutcher would be playing against type in the dramatic role, but he welcomed the challenge. He tried to emphasize that he was changing by attempting to grow a beard and working out in the gym to put more muscle onto his lean frame. Eric Bress, who codirected *The Butterfly Effect,* said he thought Kutcher initially did not seem smart enough for the role. Then Kutcher auditioned, and Bress saw no trace of the empty-headed Kelso in Kutcher. "From the moment he opened the door, I couldn't find Michael Kelso in the house," Bress says. "The first thing I noticed was that he was a very serious person. He had given so much thought to the script." [60]

Kutcher looked forward to his role as Evan Treborn, a young man who remembers an awful childhood experience involving abuse and the death of two people. The character finds a

Kutcher grew a beard for his first major dramatic role. He is shown here in a scene from The Butterfly Effect *with costar Amy Smart.*

way to return to the past and attempts to change what happened. "I liked the idea of the movie, of someone sacrificing his own happiness for someone else's," Kutcher says. "And realizing that at the end of the day he can be happy, too. I like the idea that if you change one handshake, one step . . . the reality that every single moment in your life counts. And how much neglect we throw to every moment of our lives."[61]

Enduring a Flop

In September 2003, before *The Butterfly Effect* was ready for release, *My Boss's Daughter* hit theaters. The comedy, made two years earlier, was so unimpressive that the studio had held it, waiting for a favorable time to put it before the public. Now that Kutcher's popularity was rising thanks to his relationship with Moore, the studio determined the time was right to release the movie.

Kutcher had been a coproducer of the project and was initially excited about the concept of the movie. Director David Zucker had made the farcical *Airplane!* movie and *Police Squad!* television show, but *My Boss's Daughter* lacked the cleverness of his earlier features, and the film did not turn out as well as Kutcher had hoped. Reviewer Lisa Schwarzbaum faulted the casting. "What if the leads had been played by stronger actors, rather than actor-shaped celebrities cast more for punchline interest than punch?"[62] she wondered.

No Ill Effects

Kutcher's popularity weathered the movie's poor reviews, and his celebrity status was not adversely impacted. On the movie's debut weekend, it was number one at the box office, taking in an estimated $18 million. *People* spotlighted ten questions about Kutcher's career and relationship with Moore, and in the same issue it published a negative review of the movie. Kutcher was becoming more well known as a celebrity figure than for his work as an actor or

In suitable Western dress, Kutcher attends a showing of
The Butterfly Effect with Smart at the 2004 Sundance
Film Festival.

producer, and public interest in him focused more on his personal life than on his accomplishments.

Ignoring the disappointing reviews of *My Boss's Daughter*, which had been to some extent expected, Kutcher made good use of his name recognition and the financial benefits that came with it. He had invested in the Los Angeles restaurant Dolce, and would earn more than $6 million for the seventh season of *That '70s Show.* Kutcher was a celebrity whose name added value to every project he touched.

Little *Butterfly* Effect

Kutcher had been a strong advocate of his next movie *The Butterfly Effect,* but as much as Kutcher supported the movie and liked its message, the end product did not please reviewers. When *Butterfly Effect* was released in February 2004, both the movie and Kutcher's acting were criticized. "Kutcher is the wrong actor to anchor a psychological freak-out," wrote Gleiberman in *Entertainment Weekly.* "Wearing a scruffy beard and an expression of lost-dog woe, he overacts to signify that he wants to be taken seriously."[63]

Other reviewers thought the movie was confusing and best forgotten. "The hero of this muddled thriller suffers from memory blackouts," wrote reviewer Leah Rozen in *People.* "Filmgoers who make it to the end of the turgid *Butterfly Effect* might well be advised to follow suit."[64]

His Own Philosophy

Although *That '70s Show* and *Punk'd* remained successful television shows, Kutcher's first turn as a dramatic actor did little to improve his reputation on screen. He still brought people to the theaters, however, and despite negative reviews *The Butterfly Effect* was number one at the box office the weekend it was released.

The poor reviews did not hurt Kutcher's feelings. He tried not to get too excited by the praise he heard about his career, or get too depressed by stinging criticism. If a person did not believe too many of the good comments others offered, he reasoned, the bad also could be taken with a grain of salt.

Kutcher was still tagged with the Kelso label because of his continued portrayal of the character on television, but did not mind when people did not think of him as clever. He saw their

Dabbling in Politics

During the 2004 presidential election, Kutcher did some campaigning for Democratic candidate John Kerry. His support for the candidate included traveling with him to campaign stops in Iowa and Minnesota. While traveling with Kerry, Kutcher realized that the attention the media gave to his career and personal life was nothing compared to the way a political candidate was scrutinized. "When I was on the road with [vice presidential candidate] John Edwards and John Kerry, I realized that I got it easy," he says. "Those guys get hammered!"

Quoted in Brad Pitt, "Ashton Kutcher," *Interview,* April 2005, p. 110.

Kutcher stumps for the Democrats in his home state in 2004.

low expectations as an advantage, and continued to strive to make movies with good social messages. However, he also noted that if this type of film didn't come his way he would make something that was simply entertaining in order to continue working. "I want to do socially conscious roles, roles that say something," he said. "But it's whatever floats my boat, whatever I think people want to see. It's kind of our job to entertain people, and I take that role really seriously. I like to do things that people haven't seen before, whether it's comedy, drama, action movies, thrillers." [65]

Kutcher's personal life both helped and hindered these goals. He had never been more popular, but at the same time, the type of attention he and Moore were receiving was more intrusive than flattering. As their relationship deepened, public interest in it would only become more intense.

Chapter 6

Settling In

K utcher continued to pursue his goal of entertaining the public through acting and producing. On the movie screen and television, he put effort into creating shows that had a hint of a message yet were fun to watch. He continued to work as both an actor and a producer, acting because he loved it and producing to avoid putting all his professional eggs in one basket.

While Kutcher was working to make programs and films that people wanted to watch, his personal life was also making for riveting entertainment. Rumors of marriage and pregnancy dogged his relationship with Moore, and they were the frequent subject of photos and stories in celebrity magazines and gossipy tabloids. The glare did not subside until they were married in a quiet ceremony. Whether in or out of the magazine spotlight Kutcher continued to concentrate on his multifaceted career.

Moving in Many Directions

Around the time *The Butterfly Effect* was released in early 2004, Kutcher was involved in a number of projects. He was making new episodes of *That '70s Show,* producing two television shows, and promoting *The Butterfly Effect.* He also found time to take a small role as the self-centered boyfriend of one character in *Cheaper by the Dozen.* The comedy, which starred Steve Martin and Bonnie Hunt, was a remake of an earlier film of the same name.

While his involvement in all these projects was good for Kutcher's career, it also meant he was getting only about five hours of sleep each night. He saw his fatigue as a good sign for his career. "I once read the one thing that all the people in the Fortune 500 have in common is they all work at least 60 hours a week. So I feel like I'm on pace,"[66] he said with a laugh.

Relationship a Refuge

In the midst of his hectic schedule, Kutcher found stability in his relationship with Moore. They relaxed together on holidays, and when they were both in Los Angeles he would bring Moore's daughters to school. He attended the children's soccer games, taking an interest in the things that were important in their lives.

Newly wed, Ashton Kutcher and Demi Moore attend a hurricane relief benefit in 2005. He says they share the goal of improving people's lives.

Facing the almost constant glare of publicity has been a challenge for Kutcher, but he tries to find a positive side to it.

He did not often speak publicly about his relationship with Moore, but told one interviewer, "She's everything to me. Funny, sweet, she's anything she wants to be."[67] He said they shared the goal of improving their lives and the lives of those around them.

Celebrity Glare

The press continued to love to reveal details of the relationship between the seemingly mismatched celebrities. In March 2004 it was noted that they attended Bruce Willis's birthday party together, and *People* chronicled the pair's weekend trip to Las Vegas in spring 2004. Whenever they appeared together in public, it seemed that a photographer was not far away.

Kutcher dealt with the interest in his personal life by trying to put the press out of his mind. "The trick for me is not paying attention to it," he says. "Not reading it, not buying into it and just living."[68] He saw one positive aspect to all the attention: When he went surfing for the first time, a photographer was there to capture the moment on film. He noted that while he did not like the intrusion on his privacy, he would not have otherwise had photos of that experience.

Kutcher had never imagined that his life would be so highly examined. As a producer he had success showcasing unscripted reactions on *Punk'd,* and in real life, photographers were constantly trying to capture him in unguarded moments. "There is a bizarre shift that is taking place while I've been in the acting business in the exposure and the need to write about people's relationships," he says. "The media has literally turned our lives into the show."[69]

He wished the media would respect his privacy, but realized he could not control the actions of editors, reporters, gossip columnists, and photographers. He had a philosophical attitude toward all the attention his personal life received. He knew he had nothing to hide and there was nothing he was ashamed of. He tried to look upon it as an opportunity to grow as a person, as having the spotlight on him made him try to treat others better. "The glare kind of forces you to be a good, moral human being when you may not have been one before," he says. "And I can't do anything to change it. I've tried and I'm going to continue to try. But until then, I guess I have to take it for the good and take it for the bad and live with it."[70]

Out in the Open

Kutcher and Moore were initially hesitant to speak publicly about their relationship, although they did not try to hide the fact they were together. While they had made appearances together and were often photographed as a couple, at first they did not talk openly about their feelings for each other. Moore remained mum on the topic of Kutcher until just before they were married, but as their relationship deepened Kutcher felt more comfortable discussing it in interviews. A teary Kutcher declared his love for Moore while making an appearance on *The Oprah Winfrey Show* in 2005. "I love being with her," he says. "She makes me a better person."[71]

They also had fun with the public's interest in them as a couple. As the fifteen-year difference in their ages was what caused the most discussion about their relationship, they decided to face it head-on with an appearance together on *Saturday Night Live*. Moore dressed as a very old woman, exaggerating the age difference. The joke was heightened when Kutcher pulled a set of false teeth out of her mouth. The laughter was liberating, Moore said. Making fun of the topic out in the open showed everyone that they were well aware of the age difference, and were not bothered by it in the least. The show did not stop speculation about their relationship, however. Rumors persisted that they were going to get married soon.

Guess Who

Kutcher would rather entertain people as an actor or producer than with his personal life, and still had a goal of making movies that made people look at the world a little differently. He wanted

Big Wheels

When he was growing up in Iowa, Kutcher was always a bit envious of the young men driving around in big pickup trucks with huge wheels. Soon after arriving in Hollywood, he bought a Dodge Durango. He satisfied his craving for an even bigger truck in fall 2004, when he bought a $93,000 Navistar CXT. He said the seven-ton truck was the most idiotic thing he had ever purchased, but also said it was something he had to have. "It's a weird boy's dream," he says. "So when I saw this truck in the newspaper, I knew I had to have it—it was the fulfillment of the truck I wanted as a kid."

Quoted in Brad Pitt, "Ashton Kutcher," *Interview,* April 2005, p. 110.

Kutcher fulfilled a childhood dream by buying a huge Navistar truck similar to this one.

to make movies with a message. Even though his work in this area was not always a critical success, he was proudest of the work he had done that enlightened audiences. *Guess Who,* released in April 2005, again gave him that opportunity.

The movie was a takeoff of *Guess Who's Coming to Dinner,* the 1967 classic starring Katharine Hepburn, Spencer Tracy, and Sidney Poitier. In that movie, Hepburn and Tracy, playing a middle-class couple of the day, are shocked when their daughter brings home a black fiancé. In *Guess Who,* Kutcher played the fiancé—meeting his black girlfriend's parents, with her father played by comedian Bernie Mac.

The idea for the movie came from Kutcher's friendship with Combs. "People couldn't figure out why the two of us were hanging out together," Kutcher says. "They were like, 'What's going on with these two? Why would this hip-hop guy from New York City and this farm kid from Iowa be hanging out?' They really couldn't look past the race line."[72]

Kutcher hoped the movie would help change attitudes toward race, but despite his worthy motives, the film was not a huge hit. Reviewers said it did not compare favorably to the original. The

Kutcher's and Bernie Mac's characters try to relate to each other in Guess Who, a film Kutcher hoped would raise awareness about racism.

Amanda Peet and Ashton Kutcher rehearse on the set of **A Lot Like Love**. *Kutcher's acting, and the film, were panned by critics.*

movie was criticized for being bland with its best scene coming when Kutcher tells racial jokes. "Real nerves are touched, both onscreen and with viewers," wrote Rozen. "What had been a dopey, slapsticky movie suddenly takes on a hint of substance as the characters discuss what it means to traffic in such humor and where lines are crossed."[73] The rest of the movie lacked the same tension, however, and the film got two stars as Rozen criticized Kutcher's performance as one-dimensional.

A Lot Like Love

Guess Who was followed by another lackluster showing for Kutcher. In May 2005 *A Lot Like Love* was released. In this romantic comedy Kutcher and actress Amanda Peet play a couple who are perfect for each other, but take years to realize it. The movie follows the couple over a seven-year time span, from their first

In A Lot Like Love, *Kutcher's character attempts to serenade his girlfriend.*

meeting on an airplane through her numerous break-ups and his preoccupation with work. The movie used a concept similar to the '80s hit *When Harry Met Sally,* having friendship turn into something deeper, but the script was not as polished or clever as in the earlier movie.

Kutcher's acting garnered poor reviews, and his on-screen pairing with Peet was panned. He tried to look cute and sensitive, and funny as well, but missed the mark. "They're a mutual admiration society passing themselves off as lovebirds," wrote Gleiberman, adding that "*A Lot Like Love* is a lot like a romantic comedy, except that all that's keeping these two kids apart is the trivially insufferable movie they're in." [74]

Beauty and the Geek

Kutcher barely had time to notice the negative movie reviews, however, as his career as a television producer moved smoothly along. While he faltered as an actor, his track record as a producer was bolstered by a surprise success when *Beauty and the Geek* premiered on the WB network in the summer of 2005 and captured a loyal audience.

The reality show paired eight attractive but dim-witted women with eight bright but socially inept men. They competed to see which team could learn the most from each other. The women sought to help the men become more socially adept, while the men tried to help the women increase their knowledge. Each week one couple was eliminated, and the winning couple stood to receive $250,000.

The show faced an uphill battle when it premiered. It followed the footsteps of so many reality-based competition shows, such as *American Idol, The Bachelor,* and *The Amazing Race,* that some wondered how a fresh spin could be put on the concept. There was also the fear the show would be demeaning for the contestants, and that they would end up making cruel fun of each other and their shortcomings.

A Shocking Success

The tone of the show was instructive rather than demeaning, however, and Kutcher, Goldberg, and the show's other producers were careful to avoid making it degrading. "Here's the shock: *Beauty* is sweet, funny and virtually humiliation free," wrote reviewer Robert Bianco. "Kutcher and Goldberg have dodged almost every one of the genre's negative hot buttons, and in the process they produced one of the summer's hot tickets." [75]

Typical reality television tricks, such as hot-tub scenes, hidden cameras, and commercial breaks during tense times, were used in a way that almost parodied the reality television genre. Scenes such as a beautiful young woman failing a history quiz by stating that Herbert Hoover was president during the Civil War and a rhythm-challenged genius attempting to dance proved to be funny rather than undignified. The contestants comforted each other when they lost and celebrated each small victory with gusto, giving the show a sense of camaraderie.

Kutcher tried to send a message with the show as well, that what is inside a person is what really counts, but one reviewer thought that aspect of the show went a little too far. While Terry Kelleher noted that the show "offers some fresh amusement before the gag starts wearing thin," he felt that trying to convince audiences that the contestants actually learned something from being on the show went a bit too far. "Spare us the priceless life lessons—we know you want the money,"[76] he said. Audiences and the network did not seem to mind the show's instructive overtones, however, and the program was renewed for a second season.

Fallback Career

As successful as he was as a producer, Kutcher still thought of that as his fallback career. His preferred acting to producing, even though his acting and movies were not well received and he was not overly confident in his ability. There are no reports of him investing time in acting lessons, however. Although acting was something he wanted to continue to do, if he could not succeed at it naturally he would rather prepare to do something else in the entertainment industry.

In spite of lackluster reviews for a number of his movies, Kutcher's popularity ensured him a steady stream of movie offers. He continued to think of ideas for *Punk'd* and concepts for other new shows, but did not have to worry about his acting career coming to a halt. He was still offered roles, as his celebrity status helped draw attention to even a mediocre film and his name alone could bring his fans to the theater. Kutcher realized that a big part of his job when he signed on to do a movie was to appear on talk shows, do interviews, and make publicity appearances for the movies. If

Varied Interests

Even when he is not working, Kutcher stays busy. Because he gets bored quickly, he has a variety of interests. "I like doing a lot of stuff," he says. "I love playing the piano. I love spending time with my family. I love playing basketball. I like watching the weather channel." Another interest is snowboarding. "It's good because I can go up there all by myself and put on a face mask," he says. "It's the only time I can put on a face mask and not feel like I'm robbing a store."

Kutcher also gave writing a try, although he writes more for personal satisfaction than as a career move. "As a hobby I write scripts and then throw them away," he says. "I can never seem to get the ending right. It's more a therapeutic thing. Or I'll take a pass at a script we're working on just to see if I can do it, though I never turn it in to anyone. I want these things to be just for fun."

Quoted in Rory Evans, "Ashton Kutcher, Unzipped," *GQ*, February 2004, p. 72; Ashton Kutcher, Drew Dotson, and S. Tia Brown, "Ask Ashton Anything," *Teen People*, April 1, 2005, p. 98; and Brad Pitt, "Ashton Kutcher," *Interview*, April 2005, p. 110.

Kutcher and friends (including Sean Combs and Leonardo DiCaprio) attend an NBA game in Los Angeles.

he did not agree to do this, he would not get work. Because acting was a part of his career that he loved, he put up with the rest. "I get paid to go out and sell the movie, but I'll act for free,"[77] he says.

In order to diversify his career and avoid being stereotyped into Kelso-type roles, there was one acting job Kutcher gave up: He left *That '70s Show* in 2005. It was a decision he needed to make for the good of his career, but he would miss working with friends who were with him long before he became a celebrity. "They're my best friends," he says. "They're the people I confide in. Connecting with them on a daily basis has been the greatest gift."[78]

Marriage and Fatherhood

Moore and her family became the center of Kutcher's life when their long-rumored marriage took place on September 24, 2005. As celebrities in the public eye, it was difficult for Kutcher and Moore to maintain any privacy in their relationship, but they were able to arrange a small, intimate wedding. There had been speculation for months that Kutcher and Moore were going to be married, and she coyly wore her engagement ring for a photo for the cover of *Harper's Bazaar,* but did not announce their engagement. In the interview, she offered a few comments on Kutcher, indicating that she gave him credit for accepting her, her family, and her past.

The wedding was pulled together quickly and took place in their Beverly Hills home with about one hundred friends and relatives in attendance. At the ceremony were Moore's daughters, Rumer, seventeen; Scout, fourteen; and Tallulah, eleven, as well as their father, Bruce Willis. Kutcher's costars from *That '70s Show* were there, as was Kutcher's producing partner Jason Goldberg.

Kutcher and Moore settled into a newly remodeled house. They had been staying at Kutcher's home, which was more of a bachelor pad than the one the family now shared. The redone house reflected both Moore and Kutcher's interests, with Kutcher insisting on multiple plasma televisions so he could watch numerous football games and Moore tastefully fitting them into the home's decor.

Ashton Kutcher nuzzles Demi Moore as they leave a party in Beverly Hills. Kutcher has readily embraced family life.

Family-Friendly Future

Moore's daughters effortlessly accepted Kutcher into their family. They called him MOD, short for "My Other Dad," and Kutcher reciprocated by stepping easily into the role. Kutcher and Moore have noted that they would gladly welcome the addition of more children into their family, and Kutcher loves being a father as well as a husband. His work took on a family feel as well, as he signed on to do voice work for the cartoon *Open Season.* He also had a role in the movie *Bobby,* a film about the assassination of Robert F. Kennedy in which Moore had a starring role. Another project was a movie called *The Guardian,* a drama about the Coast Guard, starring Kevin Costner. Kutcher played a rebellious young man who enlists, while Costner played a legendary rescue swimmer. Kutcher's name was also linked with more television programs, and there was even talk of a movie and sitcom based on his relationship with Moore.

Kutcher's goals are to continue to act and produce, but bringing even more diversity to his career is not out of the question. He dabbles in writing and hopes one day to direct. The young man who had once thought he would never make it out of Iowa is making quite an impact in Hollywood, enjoying it with the family he feels fortunate to be part of.

Chapter 1: Iowa Upbringing

1. Quoted in Josh Gajewski, *Profile: Ashton's Great Balancing Act,"* "*USA Weekend,* April 10, 2005. www.usaweekend.com/05_issues/050410/050410ashton_kutcher.html.
2. Quoted in *People,* "Spirit of '76," November 2, 1998, p. 75.
3. Quoted in Deanna Kizis, "Ashton Kutcher on Past Party Days and His Rock-Solid Relationship," *Cosmopolitan,* February 2001, p. 174.
4. Quoted in Carrie Bell, "Smooth Dude: Ashton Kutcher Claims He's Been 'Uncool' His Whole Life. Carrie Bell Begs to Differ," *Teen Vogue,* Spring 2001, p. 106.
5. Quoted in Brad Pitt, "Ashton Kutcher," *Interview,* April 2005, p. 110.
6. Quoted in Bell, "Smooth Dude," p. 106.
7. Ashton Kutcher, Drew Dotson, and S. Tia Brown, "Ask Ashton Anything," *Teen People,* April 1, 2005, p. 98.
8. Quoted in *People,* "Spirit of '76," p. 75.
9. Quoted in Elizabeth Weltzman, "Kutcher in the Rye," *Interview,* March 2000, p. 70.

Chapter 2: Fresh Face in Hollywood

10. Quoted in Kizis, "Ashton Kutcher on Past Party Days," p. 174.
11. Quoted in Pitt, "Ashton Kutcher," p. 110.
12. Quoted in *People,* "Spirit of '76," p. 75.
13. Quoted in Rory Evans, "Ashton Kutcher, Unzipped," *GQ,* February 2004, p. 72.
14. Quoted in Weltzman, "Kutcher in the Rye," p. 70.
15. Quoted in *People,* "Spirit of '76," p. 75.
16. Quoted in Bell, "Smooth Dude," p. 106.
17. Quoted in Weltzman, "Kutcher in the Rye," 70.
18. Quoted in *People,* "Ashton Kutcher: Actor," May 8, 2000, p. 161.

19. Quoted in Molly Lopez, "Un-Hip Ashton," *People,* April 4, 2005, p. 138.
20. James Collins, "Short Takes," *Time,* August 24, 1998, p. 82.
21. Quoted in Annie Marie Cruz, "Leave It to Seaver," *People,* February 2, 2004, p. 104.

Chapter 3: Making Dimness Pay

22. Quoted in *People,* "Spirit of '76," p. 75.
23. Quoted in *People,* "Ashton Kutcher: Actor," p. 161.
24. Quoted in Bell, "Smooth Dude," p. 106.
25. Quoted in Kizis, "Ashton Kutcher on Past Party Days," p. 174.
26. Quoted in Bell, "Smooth Dude," p. 106.
27. Quoted in Alex Lewin, "Great Expectations—Ashton Kutcher," *Premiere.* www.premiere.com/article.asp?section_id=6&article_id=574&page_number=1.
28. Quoted in Weltzman, "Kutcher in the Rye," p. 70.
29. Quoted in Weltzman, "Kutcher in the Rye," p. 70.
30. Joe Leydon, *"Dude, Where's My Car?" Variety,* December 18, 2000, p. 24.
31. Quoted in Kizis, "Ashton Kutcher on Past Party Days," p. 174.
32. Leydon, *"Dude, Where's My Car?"* p. 24.
33. Quoted in Bell, "Smooth Dude," p. 106.
34. Quoted in Kizis, "Ashton Kutcher on Past Party Days," p. 174.
35. Quoted in Kizis, "Ashton Kutcher on Past Party Days," p. 174.
36. Quoted in Weltzman, "Kutcher in the Rye," p. 70.
37. Quoted in Bell, "Smooth Dude," p. 106.

Chapter 4: Producer

38. Quoted in David Keeps et al., "The 25 Hottest Stars Under 25," *Teen People,* June 1, 2002, p. 99.
39. Quoted in *Teen People,* "What's Next," December 1, 2001, p. 17.
40. Quoted in Pitt, "Ashton Kutcher," p. 110.
41. Quoted in Pitt, "Ashton Kutcher," p. 110.
42. Quoted in Steve Garbarino, "The Joker Isn't So Wild," *TV Guide,* November 1, 2003, p. 35.
43. Quoted in Gavin Edwards, "Ashton Kutcher," *Rolling Stone,* May 29, 2003, p. 44.

44. Tom Gliatto and Frank Swertlow, "Tube," *People,* May 12, 2003, p. 27.
45. Michael Endelman, "MTV *Punk'd*: The Complete First Season," *Entertainment Weekly,* January 23, 2004, p. 89.
46. Quoted in Evans, "Ashton Kutcher, Unzipped," p.72.
47. Quoted in Anthony Breznican, "No Love at First Sight in 'Just Married,'" *Milwaukee Journal Sentinel,* January 9, 2003. www.findarticles.com/p/articles/mi_qn4196/is_20030109/ai_n10852761.
48. Owen Gleiberman, "Troth or Dare: Ashton Kutcher and Brittany Murphy Form an Imperfect Union in the Newlywed Comedy *Just Married,*" *Entertainment Weekly,* January 17, 2003, p. 54.
49. Quoted in Breznican, "No Love at First Sight."
50. Quoted in Deanna Kizis, "Achin' for Ashton," *Cosmopolitan,* April 2003, p. 138.
51. Quoted in Kizis, "Achin' for Ashton," p. 138.
52. Quoted in Kizis, "Achin' for Ashton," p. 138.

Chapter 5: New Projects, New Relationship

53. Quoted in Sarah Bailey, "Demi's Next Act," *Harper's Bazaar,* September 2005, p. 340.
54. Quoted in Jill Smolowe et al., "Summer Surprise," *People,* June 16, 2003, p. 108.
55. Quoted in Ann Oldenburg, "Fame Cozies Up to Kutcher," *USA Today,* August 19, 2003, p. 1D.
56. Quoted in Greg Adkins, "According to Ashton," *People,* January 26, 2004, p. 19.
57. Quoted in Garbarino, "The Joker Isn't So Wild," p. 37.
58. Quoted in Michelle Tauber et al., "The Real Thing!" *People,* October 10, 2005, p. 59.
59. Quoted in Kizis, "Achin' for Ashton," p. 138.
60. Quoted in Garbarino, "The Joker Isn't So Wild," p. 37.
61. Quoted in Evans, "Ashton Kutcher, Unzipped," p. 72.
62. Lisa Schwarzbaum, "*My Boss's Daughter*: Please, Somebody Pink-Slip This Manic Mess of a Comedy," *Entertainment Weekly,* September 5, 2003, p. 55.

63. Owen Gleiberman, *"The Butterfly Effect,"* *Entertainment Weekly,* February 6, 2004, p. 123.

64. Leah Rozen, *"The Butterfly Effect,"* *People,* February 2, 2004, p. 27.

65. Quoted in Brian Hiatt, *"Effect's* Heavy," *Entertainment Weekly,* January 22, 2004. www.ew.com/ew/report/0,6115,581353_21_0_,00.html.

Chapter 6: Settling In

66. Quoted in Hiatt, *"Effect's* Heavy."

67. Quoted in Garbarino, "The Joker Isn't So Wild," p. 37.

68. Quoted in *Teen People,* "5 Questions with Ashton Kutcher," June 1, 2004, p. 70.

69. Quoted in Gajewski, "Profile: Ashton's Great Balancing Act."

70. Quoted in Pitt, "Ashton Kutcher," p. 110.

71. Quoted in Michelle Tan, "The Other Dad," *People,* March 21, 2005, p. 108.

72. Quoted in Pitt, "Ashton Kutcher," p. 110.

73. Leah Rozen, "Guess Who," *People,* April 4, 2005, p. 31.

74. Owen Gleiberman, *"A Lot Like Love,"* *Entertainment Weekly,* April 29, 2005, p. 124.

75. Robert Bianco, "Sweet 'Geek' Pulls Off a Beautiful Feat," *USA Today,* June 1, 2005, p. 3D.

76. Terry Kelleher, *"Beauty and the Geek*: WB," *People,* June 6, 2005, p. 37.

77. Quoted in Pitt, "Ashton Kutcher," p. 110.

78. Kutcher, Dotson, and Brown, "Ask Ashton Anything," p. 98.

1978

Christopher Ashton Kutcher is born on February 7 in Cedar Rapids, Iowa.

1996

Kutcher graduates from high school and enrolls at the University of Iowa.

1997

A talent scout spots Kutcher in a bar and encourages him to enter a modeling competition. He wins a trip to New York, lands an agent and begins his modeling career.

1998

Heading to Hollywood, Kutcher is offered two roles on his first day there. He accepts a part in *That '70s Show* and gains recognition after the series debuts in the fall.

1999

Kutcher makes his first movie, the Western *Texas Rangers,* and also has a small role in *Coming Soon.*

2000

Reindeer Games and *Down to You* are released, and Kutcher has small roles in both. At the end of the year he hits it big as one of the leads in *Dude, Where's My Car?* The goofy comedy is popular with high school and college students.

2001

Kutcher stars in and is one of the producers of *The Guest,* which is retitled *My Boss's Daughter* when it is released two years later.

2002

Films the romantic comedy *Just Married* with Brittany Murphy. After filming ends, he begins a romantic relationship with his costar that lasts seven months.

2003

Punk'd debuts and is a hit. Kutcher produces the show, which involves pranks played on his celebrity friends. Kutcher also films the drama *The Butterfly Effect*. He begins dating actress Demi Moore and is named America's hottest bachelor by *People*.

2004

The Butterfly Effect is released, and Kutcher takes a small role in *Cheaper by the Dozen*, a comedy starring Steve Martin.

2005

Kutcher stars in the movies *Guess Who* and *A Lot Like Love*. He produces the television show *Beauty and the Geek*. On September 24 he marries actress Demi Moore.

2006

Kutcher plans to do voice work for the cartoon *Open Season*, and takes a small role in the movie *Bobby*, a film about the assassination of Robert F. Kennedy in which Moore has a starring role. He also travels to Louisiana and North Carolina to make *The Guardian*, a movie about the Coast Guard that stars Kevin Costner.

For Further Reading

Books

Grace Norwich, *Ashton!* New York: Simon Spotlight, 2003. This paperback offers color photos of Ashton Kutcher and a look at his work in *That '70s Show* and *Punk'd.*

Marc Shapiro, *Ashton Kutcher: The Life and Loves of the King of "Punk'd."* New York: Pocket Books, 2004. A fan-oriented paperback outlining Ashton Kutcher's life.

Jennifer Torres, *Ashton Kutcher.* Hockessin, DE: Michell Lane, 2006. An easy-to-read narrative of Ashton Kutcher's life.

Periodicals

Sarah Bailey, "Demi's Next Act," *Harper's Bazaar.* September 2005.

Steve Garbarino, "The Joker Isn't So Wild," *TV Guide*, November 11, 2003.

Michelle Tauber, et al. "The Real Thing," *People,* October 10, 2005.

Web Sites

"Ashton Kutcher," Internet Movie Database. www.imdb.com/name/nm0005110/. A brief biography of Kutcher and an updated list of his film work.

Eonline. www.eonline.com. A search for Ashton Kutcher brings up a list of his movies and articles about him.

People. www.people.com. The comings and goings of Kutcher and other celebrities are noted on the online home of *People.* Search for Kutcher to find the latest information on his life.

Punk'd. MTV. www.mtv.com/onair/dyn/punkd/series.jhtml. Information on *Punk'd* episodes, video clips, and behind-the-scenes tidbits from Kutcher.

TV.com. www.tv.com. Search for *That '70s Show* to find episode summaries for the series.

Abercrombie and Fitch, 30, 39

A Lot Like Love (film), 83–85

Barnett, Amy, 66
Beauty and the Geek (TV series), 12, 85–86
Bianco, Robert, 85
Bobby (film), 90
Butterfly Effect, The (film), 69–71, 73

Cameron, Kirk, 17
Cedar Rapids (Iowa), 14, 19, 23, 28
Cheaper by the Dozen (film), 76
Clear Creek Amana High School, 20
Combs, Sean "P. Diddy," 60, 66, 68
Coming Soon (film), 39
Cook, Rachel Leigh, 40
Cosmopolitan (magazine), 46, 60
Costner, Kevin, 90

Derek, Bo, 31, 34
Dorff, Stephen, 56
Down to You (film), 39
Dude, Where's My Car? (film), 10, 42–43

Entertainment Weekly (magazine), 41, 73

Gleiberman, Owen, 58, 73, 85
Goldberg, Jason, 52, 54
Guardian, The (film), 90
Guess Who (film), 82–83

Hanson (pop band), 46
Hunt, Bonnie, 76

Interview (magazine), 30, 36

Jones, January, 39
Just Married (film), 57–58

Kelso, Michael (TV character), 32, 42, 63, 70
  popularity of, 33, 36–37
  stereotype of, 73, 88
Kerry, John, 74
Kunis, Mila, 37–38
Kutcher, (Christopher) Ashton
  on celebrity, 45–46, 79–80
  in college, 23–28
  on comedy, 33
  early auditions of, 31–32
  early life of, 14–19
  as "Fresh Face of Iowa," 28–29

in high school, 20–23
on similarities with Kelso, 32
marriage of, 88
modeling career of, 30
pastimes of, 87
as producer, 48–50, 85
Kutcher, Diane (mother), 14, 15, 19
Kutcher, Larry (father), 14, 15
Kutcher, Michael (brother), 14, 16, 18
Kutcher, Tausha (sister), 14, 21, 28

Lachey, Nick, 55
Leiner, Danny, 42
Levy, Shawn, 65
Leydon, Joe, 42
Link, Greg, 68

Mac, Bernie, 82
Martin, Denise, 54
Martin, Steve, 76
Masterson, Danny, 37, 38
McDermott, Dylan, 40
Miner, Steve, 41
Moore, Demi, 13, 76, 77, 79
early relationship between Ashton and, 63–68
marries Ashton, 88–90
Moore, Freddy, 64
Muniz, Frankie, 55
Murphy, Brittany, 57–61

My Boss's Daughter (film), 51, 71–72

Open Season (animated film), 90
Oprah Winfrey Show, The (TV series), 80
Osbourne, Kelly, 56

Peet, Amanda, 83
People (magazine), 37, 41, 73
on relationship with Demi Moore, 66, 71, 79
on success of Punk'd, 54–55
Philbin, Regis, 34
Pink, 55
Pitt, Brad, 81
Porter, Kim, 66
Portwood, Mark, 19
Prinze, Freddie, Jr., 39–40
Punk'd (TV series), 11, 12, 73
Ashton creates concept for, 51–56
unaired episode of, 57

Reid, Tara, 49, 51
Reindeer Games (film), 39
Rodriguez, Alex, 57
Rolling Stone (magazine), 60
Rozen, Leah, 73

Schwarzbaum, Lisa, 71
Scott, Ashley, 59

Scott, Seann William, 42
Seventeen (magazine), 41
Simon, Stephanie, 35
Simpson, Jessica, 55
Stiles, Julia, 39–40

Teen People (magazine), 66
Texas Rangers (film), 39–40, 46
That '70s Show (TV series), 10, 32, 36, 73
Timberlake, Justin, 52, 56
Turner, Bonnie, 33
Turner, Terry, 33

University of Iowa, 23, 28, 34

Valderrama, Wilmer, 38
Van Der Beek, James, 40
Variety (magazine), 42

Weltzman, Elizabeth, 30
Who Wants to Be a Millionaire? (TV series), 34
Willis, Bruce, 64, 66–67, 79
Wind on Water (TV series), 31

Zucker, David, 71

Terri Dougherty is a newspaper reporter who enjoys writing biographies as well as other books for children. *Ashton Kutcher* is her ninth People in the News biography. She lives in Appleton, Wisconsin, with her husband, Denis, and their three children, Kyle, Rachel, and Emily.